D0624374

I want to be a Pilot

I WANT TO BE A

Pilot

DAN LIEBMAN

FIREFLY BOOKS

A FIREFLY BOOK

Published by Firefly Books Ltd. 1999

Copyright © 1999 Firefly Books Ltd.

All rights reserved. No part of this publication may be reproduced, stored in a retrieval system or transmitted in any form or by any means, electronic, mechanical, photocopying, recording or otherwise, without the written permission of the publisher.

Sixth printing, 2014

Library and Archives Canada Cataloguing in Publication

Main entry under title:
I want to be a pilot
ISBN-13: 978-1-55209-499-5 (bound)
ISBN-10: 1-55209-449-9 (bound)
ISBN-13: 978-1-55209-434-1 (pbk.)
ISBN-10: 1-55209-434-0 (pbk.)
1. Air pilots - Juvenile literature.
2. Aeronautics - Juvenile literature.
TL547.I25   1999   j629.13
C99-930931-5

Published in Canada by
Firefly Books Ltd.
50 Staples Avenue, Unit 1
Richmond Hill, Ontario L4B 0A7

Publisher Cataloging-in-Publication Data (U.S.)

I want to be a pilot / [Firefly Books Ltd.].–1st ed/
[24] p. : col. ill. ; cm. –I want to be.
Summary: Photos and easy-to-read text about
the job of an air pilot.
ISBN-13: 978-1-55209-449-5 (bound)
ISBN-10: 1-55209-449-9 (bound)
ISBN-13: 978-1-55209-434-1 (pbk.)
ISBN-10: 1-55209-434-0 (pbk.)
1. Air pilots – Vocational guidance – Juvenile
literature.
[1. Air pilots – Vocational guidance.   2. Occupations.]
I. Title.   II. Series.
331.761/6291–dc21   1999   AC   CIP

Published in the United States by
Firefly Books (U.S.) Inc.
P.O. Box 1338, Ellicott Station
Buffalo, New York 14205

Photo Credits

© Tony Cassanova, front cover
© William Boyce/CORBIS, page 5
© Morton Beebe/CORBIS, page 6
© Vince Streano/CORBIS, page 7
© Roger Ressmeyer/CORBIS, pages 8-9
© George Hall/CORBIS, pages 10, 11, 19, 24
© Jim Sugar/CORBIS, pages 12-13, 22-23
© Reuters/CORBIS, page 14

© Graham Wheatley; The Military Picture
Library/CORBIS, page 15
© Leif Skoogfors/CORBIS, page 16
© CORBIS SYGMA, page 17
© Ron Watts/CORBIS, page 18
© Firefly Productions/CORBIS, page 20
© Bill Varie/CORBIS, page 21
© Bob Krist/CORBIS, back cover

Design by Interroband Graphic Design Inc.
Manufactured by Printplus Limited in Shen Zhen, Guang Dong, P.R. China in December 2014,
Job #S141200268.

The publisher acknowledges the financial support of the Government of Canada through the Book Publishing Industry Development Program for its publishing activities.

Some pilots fly small planes. This float plane ties up to a dock – just like a boat does.

Other pilots fly jumbo planes that take people to faraway places.

Large airplanes have many dials and gagets in front of the pilots. One dial shows how fast the plane is flying.

Two pilots guide their plane down for a landing. Pilots sit in a cabin called the cockpit.

Fighter planes like this one fly high above the clouds. Only very experienced pilots get to fly them.

When planes fly this high, there is not enough air to breathe. That's why the pilot wears a mask with a hose. The hose is connected to an air tank.

The best pilots are sometimes picked to fly at air shows. A group of planes is called a squadron. Air shows are thrilling to watch.

Pilots carry equipment as well as people. The pilot of this helicopter is trained to put out forest fires.

Some helicopters are big enough to carry people long distances. This helicopter can land on water.

There are always new safety rules for pilots to learn.

Fighter planes are used in the air force. They have only a small cabin. A pilot must lower himself or herself carefully down.

Every airport has a control tower. The people who work in the tower tell pilots when it is safe to take off and to land.

The navigator is part of the air crew. Navigators check the position of the plane in the sky.

It only seems like this pilot is in the sky. He's really on the ground – training to fly at night.

This pilot is carefully checking his plane before takeoff to make sure it is safe.

It takes a lot of training to be a pilot, but the hard work pays off. For a pilot, every new flight is a new adventure.